GIANT DINOSAURS
Sauropods

Clare Hibbert

Enslow Publishing
101 W. 23rd Street
Suite 240
New York, NY 10011
USA

enslow.com

Published in 2019 by Enslow Publishing, LLC
101 W. 23rd Street, Suite 240, New York, NY 10011

Cataloging-in-Publication Data

Names: Hibbert, Clare.
Title: Giant Dinosaurs: Sauropods / Clare Hibbert.
Description: New York : Enslow Publishing, 2019. | Series: Dino explorers | Includes glossary
and index.
Identifiers: ISBN 9780766099975 (pbk.) | ISBN 9780766099968 (library bound) | ISBN
9780766099999 (6 pack.) | ISBN 9780766099982 (ebook)
Subjects: LCSH: Saurischia--Juvenile literature. | Dinosaurs--Juvenile literature.
Classification: LCC QE862.S3 H53 2019 | DDC 567.913--dc23

Printed in the United States of America

To Our Readers: We have done our best to make sure all website addresses
in this book were active and appropriate when we went to press. However,
the author and the publisher have no control over and assume no
liability for the material available on those websites or on any websites
they may link to. Any comments or suggestions can be sent by email to
customerservice@enslow.com.

Excerpts and articles have been reproduced with the permission of the
copyright holders.

CONTENTS

The Dinosaur Age

Dinosaurs appeared around 225 million years ago (mya) and ruled the land for over 160 million years. At the same time (the Mesozoic Era), marine reptiles and pterosaurs ruled the oceans and skies.

Dinosaurs

This family tree shows when various dinosaurs appeared and how they were related. As new fossils are found, paleontologists often change their minds about the groupings.

Dinosaurs suddenly died out 65 mya, along with marine reptiles, pterosaurs and many other animals. A huge meteorite probably hit Earth, throwing up dust that blocked out the Sun for months.

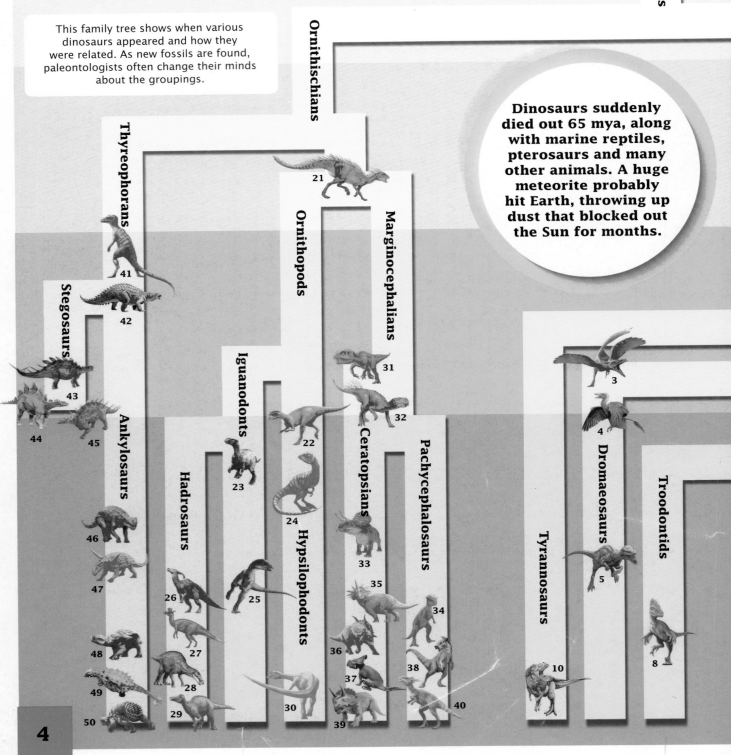

Ornithischians

Thyreophorans

Ornithopods

Marginocephalians

Stegosaurs

Iguanodonts

Ceratopsians

Pachycephalosaurs

Ankylosaurs

Hadrosaurs

Hypsilophodonts

Tyrannosaurs

Dromaeosaurs

Troodontids

KEY

1. *Herrerasaurus*
2. *Allosaurus*
3. *Archaeopteryx*
4. *Microraptor*
5. *Deinonychus*
6. *Spinosaurus*
7. *Giganotosaurus*
8. *Troodon*
9. *Therizinosaurus*
10. *Tyrannosaurus*
11. *Melanorosaurus*
12. *Plateosaurus*
13. *Mamenchisaurus*
14. *Brachiosaurus*
15. *Amargasaurus*
16. *Nigersaurus*
17. *Sauroposeidon*
18. *Argentinosaurus*
19. *Saltasaurus*
20. *Rapetosaurus*
21. *Heterodontosaurus*
22. *Hypsilophodon*
23. *Iguanodon*
24. *Leaellynasaura*
25. *Gasparinisaura*
26. *Parasaurolophus*
27. *Lambeosaurus*
28. *Shantungosaurus*
29. *Edmontosaurus*
30. *Thescelosaurus*
31. *Yinlong*
32. *Psittacosaurus*
33. *Zuniceratops*
34. *Stegoceras*
35. *Styracosaurus*
36. *Achelousaurus*
37. *Protoceratops*
38. *Pachycephalosaurus*
39. *Triceratops*
40. *Stygimoloch*
41. *Scutellosaurus*
42. *Scelidosaurus*
43. *Tuojiangosaurus*
44. *Stegosaurus*
45. *Kentrosaurus*
46. *Minmi*
47. *Sauropelta*
48. *Edmontonia*
49. *Euoplocephalus*
50. *Ankylosaurus*

Saurischians

Theropods

Therizinosaurs

Allosaurs

Spinosaurs

Sauropods

Titanosaurs

Diplodocids

Prosauropods

Triassic
251–206 mya

Jurassic
206–145 mya

Cretaceous
145–65 mya

Melanorosaurus

One of the earliest sauropods, or long-necked plant-eating dinosaurs, *Melanorosaurus* lived between 227 and 208 mya. Its name means "Black Mountain lizard" after the place where it was first discovered: Black Mountain in Transkei, South Africa.

First of the Line

In time, sauropods would become the largest land animals ever. Early species were much smaller—*Melanorosaurus* was just a quarter the length of *Argentinosaurus* (pages 20–21) and far lighter. However, it was still too bulky to walk on two legs and had to lumber along on all fours.

Volcanoes were reshaping the land during the Late Triassic.

All in the Hips

Sauropods belong to the dinosaur group called the saurischians, or lizard-hipped dinosaurs. Their hips were arranged like those of modern lizards. Sauropods were plant-eaters, but the meat-eating theropods were lizard-hipped, too. The other group of dinosaurs are the ornithischians, or bird-hipped dinosaurs. They were all plant-eaters.

ornithischian   saurischian

Melanorosaurus's long neck allowed it to save energy. It could gather vegetation from a large area without the need to move its whole body.

Name: *Melanorosaurus*
(Mel-uh-NOR-uh-SAWR-us)
Family: Melanorosauridae
Height: 14 feet (4.3 m)
Length: 26 feet (8 m)
Weight: 1.4 tons (1.3 t)

DINOSAUR PROFILE

Melanosaurus weighed less than a hippo. *Argentinosaurus* was about sixty times heavier.

A long, tapering, and flexible tail helped *Melanorosaurus* to keep its balance.

Melanorosaurus had a slightly pointed skull, about 10 inches (25 cm) long.

Plateosaurus

Since the first fossils were discovered in 1834, *Plateosaurus* has been reconstructed in many ways. It has been shown with its limbs sticking out from its sides like an iguana's and—correctly—with them starting from directly under its body.

Walking the Walk

Experts have also puzzled over whether *Plateosaurus* was quadrupedal (walking on four legs) or bipedal (walking on two). Today, most agree that this European dinosaur was bipedal. Standing on two legs gave it an advantage, because it could reach high in the trees for vegetation.

Plateosaurus's long, narrow jaw had wide, serrated teeth that could shear through tough plant stems.

Compared to other prosauropods, *Plateosaurus* had short arms.

Prosauropods

Plateosaurus belonged to a group called the prosauropods, sauropods' earliest relatives. They walked on two legs, whereas the later, larger sauropods had to walk on four. Some paleontologists think prosauropods also had a more varied diet, and ate some meat as well as plants. *Melanorosaurus* (pages 6–7) used to be classed as prosauropod, too.

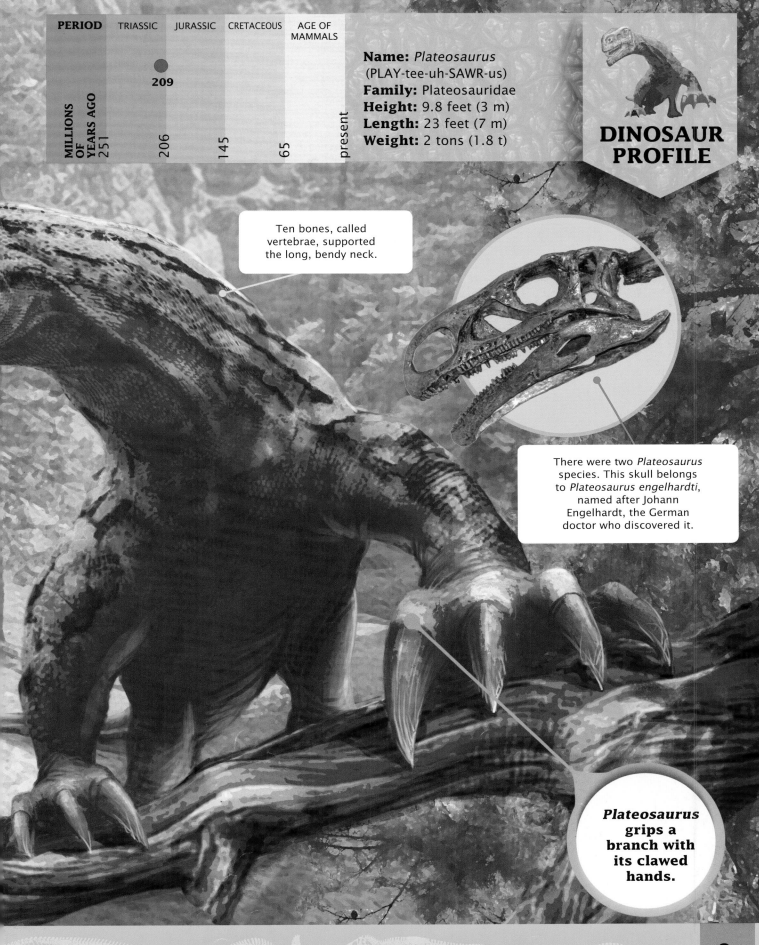

PERIOD	TRIASSIC	JURASSIC	CRETACEOUS	AGE OF MAMMALS

209

MILLIONS OF YEARS AGO

251 — 206 — 145 — 65 — present

Name: *Plateosaurus*
(PLAY-tee-uh-SAWR-us)
Family: Plateosauridae
Height: 9.8 feet (3 m)
Length: 23 feet (7 m)
Weight: 2 tons (1.8 t)

DINOSAUR PROFILE

Ten bones, called vertebrae, supported the long, bendy neck.

There were two *Plateosaurus* species. This skull belongs to *Plateosaurus engelhardti*, named after Johann Engelhardt, the German doctor who discovered it.

Plateosaurus grips a branch with its clawed hands.

Mamenchisaurus

Mamenchisaurus lived in what is now China between 160 and 145 mya. So far, seven species have been discovered. They vary greatly in size but all share one characteristic—an extra-long neck that makes up around half of their total body length.

Great and Small

The first *Mamenchisaurus* fossils, found in the 1950s, belonged to a species called *Mamenchisaurus constructus* (the *constructus* part of the name came from it being discovered on a building site). The record-breaker of the family was named in the 1990s. Known as *Mamenchisaurus sinocanadorum*, it was three times as long, with a body length of 115 feet (35 m) and a 59-foot (18-m) neck.

Hunters such as *Yangchuanosaurus* had to team up to bring down a *Mamenchisaurus*.

Mamenchisaurus's main predator was an *allosaur* called *Yangchuanosaurus*.

PERIOD	TRIASSIC	JURASSIC	CRETACEOUS	AGE OF MAMMALS
		153		
MILLIONS OF YEARS AGO	251	206	145	65	present

Name: *Mamenchisaurus*
(Mah-MEN-chih-SAWR-us)
Family: Mamenchisauridae
Height: 40 feet (12 m)
Length: 115 feet (35)
Weight: 13 tons (12 t)

DINOSAUR PROFILE

Reaching Out

Mamenchisaurus's long neck could have reached up high, but most experts believe that this dinosaur fed mostly on low-lying vegetation. Having a long neck was still an advantage. *Mamenchisaurus* could reach out for food across a large area without having to use up energy moving its body from place to place.

No one can be sure what noises sauropods made.

Mamenchisaurus could rear up to frighten off predators.

A small group of *Mamenchisaurus* go to the river to drink. Like all sauropods, this dinosaur lived in herds.

Brachiosaurus

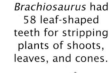

When it was discovered in 1903, *Brachiosaurus* was the largest known dinosaur. Paleontologists did not believe that such an enormous animal could have supported its own weight on land. They thought that it must have lived in water.

Nose Knowhow

In early reconstructions, *Brachiosaurus*'s nostrils were located on a bump between its eyes, where they could be used to breathe even when the rest of the head was submerged. Today, paleontologists know *Brachiosaurus* lived on land, not water, and position the nostrils further down the snout. The nostrils were relatively large, so the dinosaur probably had a good sense of smell.

Brachiosaurus had 58 leaf-shaped teeth for stripping plants of shoots, leaves, and cones.

Eating Machines

Just like today's large herbivores, sauropods moved in herds, constantly eating and seeking out new feeding grounds. Experts estimate that *Brachiosaurus* consumed 264 pounds (120 kg) of vegetation a day. Despite this, it shared its environment with other plant-eating giants, including *Apatosaurus* and *Diplodocus*.

PERIOD	TRIASSIC	JURASSIC	CRETACEOUS	AGE OF MAMMALS

152

MILLIONS OF YEARS AGO

251 | 206 | 145 | 65 | present

Name: *Brachiosaurus*
(BRACK-ee-uh-SAWR-us)
Family: Brachiosauridae
Height: 30 feet (9 m)
Length: 98 feet (30 m)
Weight: 77 tons (70 t)

DINOSAUR PROFILE

Unlike other sauropods, *Brachiosaurus* had longer front legs than back ones. Its back sloped down toward the tail.

Brachiosaurus held its neck upright, like a giraffe. One early species has since been renamed *Giraffatitan*.

Brachiosaurus lived in Late Jurassic North America.

Brachiosaurus's huge bulk helped it to conserve its body heat.

Amargasaurus

One of the smallest sauropods, 33-foot- (10-m-) long *Amargasaurus* lived around 125 mya in what is now Argentina. The sharp spines along its neck and back might have been to defend against predators or for showing off to rivals or mates.

Double Find

Amargasaurus was found on an expedition led by the Argentinian paleontologist José Bonaparte. The team discovered an almost complete skeleton. They found another dinosaur on that trip: the Late Cretaceous predator *Carnotaurus*. Like *Amargasaurus*, it is known from only one skeleton.

One theory is that *Amargasaurus*'s spines supported sails of skin that helped to keep its temperature steady.

The one *Amargasaurus* skeleton was discovered in 1984.

Feeding Strategy

Amargasaurus is one of the dicraeosaurids. The family is named after *Dicraeosaurus*, a small sauropod of Late Jurassic Tanzania, eastern Africa. Being smaller than other sauropods meant that dicraeosaurids did not have to compete for plants. They were browsing for vegetation at a different level.

Amargasaurus's broad snout was lined with long, cylinder-shaped teeth.

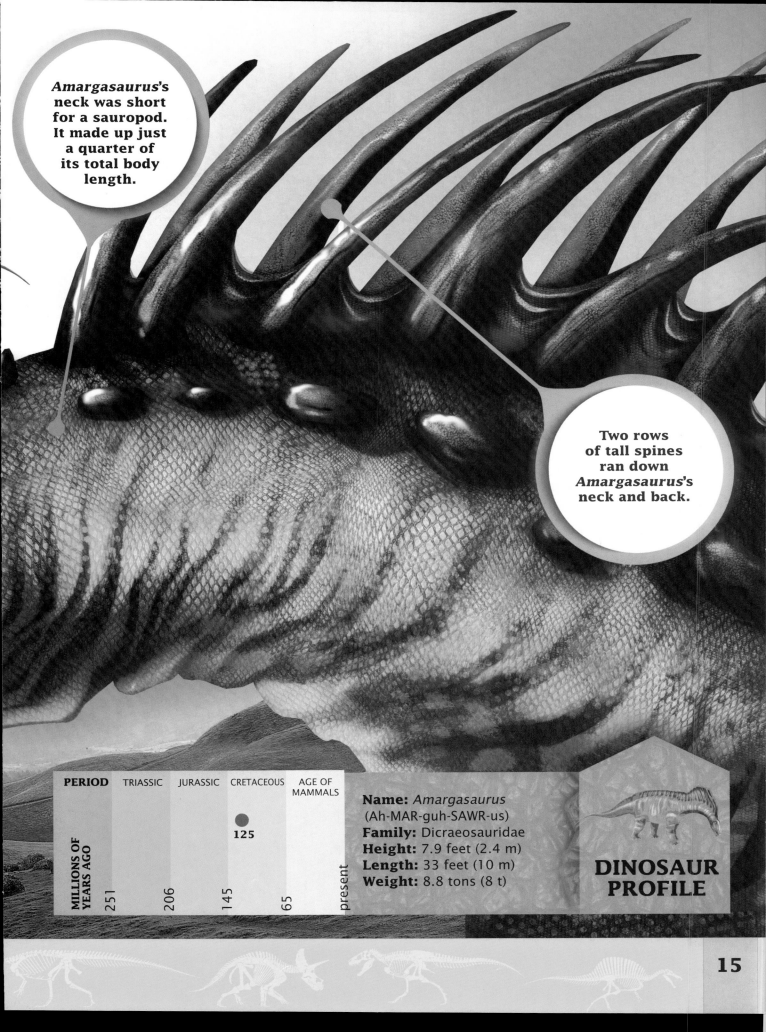

Amargasaurus's neck was short for a sauropod. It made up just a quarter of its total body length.

Two rows of tall spines ran down Amargasaurus's neck and back.

PERIOD	TRIASSIC	JURASSIC	CRETACEOUS	AGE OF MAMMALS
MILLIONS OF YEARS AGO	251	206	145 · 125	65 · present

Name: *Amargasaurus*
(Ah-MAR-guh-SAWR-us)
Family: Dicraeosauridae
Height: 7.9 feet (2.4 m)
Length: 33 feet (10 m)
Weight: 8.8 tons (8 t)

DINOSAUR PROFILE

Nigersaurus

Named after the West African country where it had been discovered in the 1970s, *Nigersaurus* was an unusual, elephant-sized sauropod. Its fossilized remains were found in the Sahara Desert, but in the Early Cretaceous this landscape was a great floodplain with rivers and lush vegetation.

Tooth Talk

Nigersaurus's straight-edged snout was packed with more than 500 teeth for munching on low-growing plants. At least 50 tiny teeth lined the front of its mouth—with about eight rows of replacement teeth behind them, ready and waiting. Cutting through fibrous vegetation was a tough job. Each tooth lasted only a couple of weeks.

Having teeth at the front of the muzzle allowed *Nigersaurus* to "mow" plants close to the ground.

PERIOD	TRIASSIC	JURASSIC	CRETACEOUS	AGE OF MAMMALS
			● 110	
MILLIONS OF YEARS AGO	251	206	145	65	present

Name: *Nigersaurus*
(NI-juh-SAWR-us)
Family: Rebbachisauridae
Height: 6.2 feet (1.9 m)
Length: 30 feet (9 m)
Weight: 4.4 tons (4 t)

DINOSAUR PROFILE

Fellow Fossils

Nigersaurus was found in the Elrhaz Formation, a band of Early Cretaceous rock in Niger, Central Africa. Other dinosaurs discovered there include the fish-eating spinosaur *Suchomimus* and the hadrosaur *Ouranosaurus*. The super-crocodile *Sarcosuchus* is also known from the Elrhaz Formation.

Nigersaurus kept its head close to the ground, raising it only to look for predators.

Nigersaurus's snout broadened out at the end.

Nigersaurus had huge eyes for a sauropod, but its nostrils were small. It probably had a poor sense of smell.

Nigersaurus fed on mosses, ferns, and other plants.

Sauroposeidon

In 1994, a few fossilized neck bones were discovered by a dog walker in Oklahoma. They belonged to *Sauroposeidon*. At 59 feet (18 m) high, it was the tallest known dinosaur, and almost as heavy as *Argentinosaurus* (pages 20–21).

Hot and Humid

Herbivorous *Sauroposeidon* lived around the shores of what is now the Gulf of Mexico 110 mya. At that time, the landscape was made up of rainforests, river deltas, and wetlands. The climate was tropical (hot and humid all year round) or subtropical (with hot, wet summers and short, mild winters).

Swampy Habitat

Sauroposeidon was named after Poseidon—the Greek god of earthquakes as well as the sea—because its huge bulk would have made the ground shake. *Sauroposeidon* was the only large sauropod around at that time. The top predator was *Acrocanthosaurus*, which preyed on young *Sauroposeidon* whenever it had the opportunity.

Fossilized *Sauroposeidon* footprints have been found in Texas.

Like other sauropods, *Sauroposeidon* lived in herds.

PERIOD	TRIASSIC	JURASSIC	CRETACEOUS	AGE OF MAMMALS	
MILLIONS OF YEARS AGO	251	206	145	65	present

110

Name: *Sauroposeidon*
(SAWR-oh-puh-SIGH-don)
Family: Titanosauridae
Height: 59 feet (18 m)
Length: 112 feet (34 m)
Weight: 60 tons (54 t)

The estimated neck length was 39 feet (12 m). The largest bone, or vertebra, was 4 feet (1.2 m) long!

Vegetation included palms, tree ferns, and magnolias.

Sauroposeidon juveniles may have lived with the herd for protection.

Argentinosaurus

The area that is now South America was warm and wet at the end of the Cretaceous, and home to some enormous, plant-eating dinosaurs. *Argentinosaurus* ("Argentina lizard") was one of the largest animals to have ever lived on land. Each of its vertebrae (spine bones) was almost as tall as a person.

Its long neck allowed the dinosaur to reach for food without moving much.

This unnamed titanosaur was even bigger than *Argentinosaurus*—as tall as a seven-story building!

Record-Breakers

A farmer found the first *Argentinosaurus* fossil by accident in 1987. At first, he mistook the massive leg bone for a petrified tree trunk. *Argentinosaurus* was a record-breaker for more than two decades, until a new species of titanosaur was discovered. Still unnamed, it was 131 feet (40 m) long, 66 feet (20 m) tall, and weighed 85 tons (77 t).

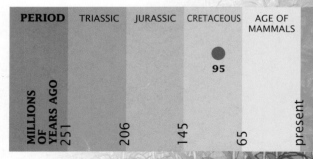

PERIOD	TRIASSIC	JURASSIC	CRETACEOUS	AGE OF MAMMALS
MILLIONS OF YEARS AGO	251	206	145	65	present

95

Name: *Argentinosaurus*
(AH-gen-teen-uh-SAWR-us)
Family: Antarctosauridae
Height: 24 feet (7.3 m)
Length: 115 feet (35 m)
Weight: 80 tons (73 t)

DINOSAUR PROFILE

Titanosaur Teeth

Argentinosaurus belonged to the group of sauropods called the titanosaurs that flourished after the large Jurassic sauropods had died out. Their nostrils were set high on the snout, and they had a jaw packed with peg-like teeth.

Argentinosaurus probably couldn't raise its neck much above shoulder height.

The long tail stuck out behind for balance.

***Argentinosaurus* may have taken 40 years to reach its adult size.**

Thick, sturdy legs supported its heavy bulk.

Saltasaurus

Saltasaurus was a titanosaur that lived in herds in Argentina at the end of the Cretaceous. When this dinosaur was discovered, it was the first sauropod known to have bony bumps, called osteoderms, on its skin. These may have helped to protect *Saltasaurus*, which was relatively small for a sauropod.

Saltasaurus had small feet and short, stubby legs.

Titanosaur Nursery

A *Saltasaurus* nesting site was discovered in Argentina in 1997. The dinosaurs had used it for hundreds of years. Most of the time, the female *Saltasaurus* laid their eggs, the eggs hatched, and the youngsters left the site. However, the site was on a floodplain. Every so often the river flooded and eggs were buried in the mud and fossilized.

Saltasaurus did not guard its nest, but may have covered it with earth or plants to keep the eggs warm and hidden from predators.

PERIOD	TRIASSIC	JURASSIC	CRETACEOUS	AGE OF MAMMALS
MILLIONS OF YEARS AGO	251	206	145	65	present

70

Name: *Saltasaurus* (Salt-uh-SAWR-us)
Family: Saltasauridae
Height: 16.4 feet (5 m)
Length: 40 feet (12 m)
Weight: 7.7 tons (7 t)

DINOSAUR PROFILE

Saltasaurus's head was supported on a small neck. The tail was short, too.

Skin Story

Saltasaurus's species name, *loricatus*, means "protected by plates." Its skin had osteoderms in two sizes. The larger ones were 4.7 inches (12 cm) long and oval. Between these were small, round ones, just 0.3 inches (0.7 cm) across. Paleontologists now know of other sauropods with osteoderms, such as 60-foot- (18-m-) long *Laplatasaurus*, also from Late Cretaceous Argentina.

There is only one known species of *Saltasaurus*: *Saltasaurus loricatus*.

Saltasaurus ate around 452 pounds (205 kg) of plant matter a day.

Rapetosaurus

Many titanosaurs are known from only a few bones, but *Rapetosaurus*'s fossils included a nearly complete skeleton. This dinosaur lived 70 mya on the island of Madagascar, off the east coast of Africa.

Stomach Stones

Like all sauropods, *Rapetosaurus* did not chew its food properly. Instead, it swallowed stones called gastroliths to grind up the plant food in its stomach.

These gastroliths were smoothed and polished inside a dinosaur's stomach.

Rapetosaurus had bony bumps, called osteoderms, on its skin.

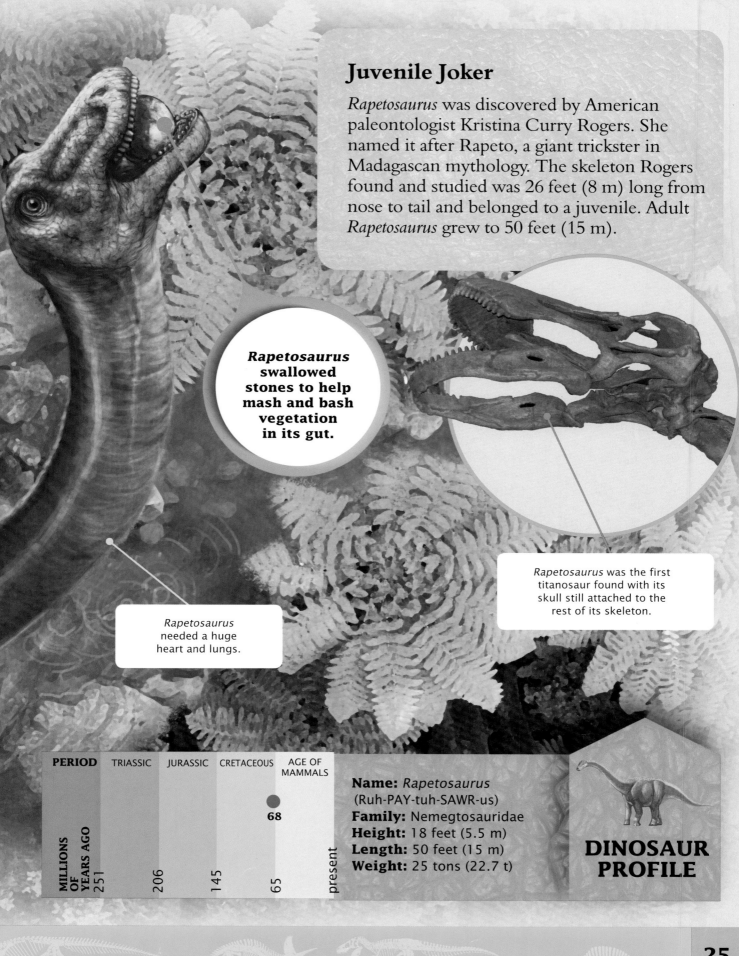

Juvenile Joker

Rapetosaurus was discovered by American paleontologist Kristina Curry Rogers. She named it after Rapeto, a giant trickster in Madagascan mythology. The skeleton Rogers found and studied was 26 feet (8 m) long from nose to tail and belonged to a juvenile. Adult *Rapetosaurus* grew to 50 feet (15 m).

Rapetosaurus swallowed stones to help mash and bash vegetation in its gut.

Rapetosaurus was the first titanosaur found with its skull still attached to the rest of its skeleton.

Rapetosaurus needed a huge heart and lungs.

PERIOD	TRIASSIC	JURASSIC	CRETACEOUS	AGE OF MAMMALS
			68	

MILLIONS OF YEARS AGO 251 206 145 65 present

Name: *Rapetosaurus* (Ruh-PAY-tuh-SAWR-us)
Family: Nemegtosauridae
Height: 18 feet (5.5 m)
Length: 50 feet (15 m)
Weight: 25 tons (22.7 t)

DINOSAUR PROFILE

Fun Facts

Now that you have discovered some amazing giant dinosaurs, boost your knowledge with these 10 quick facts about them!

Two close relatives of *Melanorosaurus* lived in the Late Triassic, too: *Eucnemesaurus*, also from South Africa, and *Riojasaurus* from South America.

Plateosaurus is one of the best-known dinosaurs. More than 100 of its skeletons have been found and studied.

One species of *Mamenchisaurus* is thought to have had a defensive tail club.

Brachiosaurus means "arm lizard." The name comes from it having longer front legs, or arms.

Amargasaurus was found at a place in Argentina called La Amarga Arroyo. Its name means "lizard from La Amarga."

The smallest *Nigersaurus* fossil is a jawbone that belonged to a tiny hatchling. It is less than 1 inch (2.5 cm) across.

Sauroposeidon may have had a close cousin. Giant vertebrae were discovered in England in 2004.

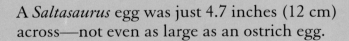

Argentinosaurus eggs were about the size of rugby balls.

A *Saltasaurus* egg was just 4.7 inches (12 cm) across—not even as large as an ostrich egg.

One *Rapetosaurus* fossil is of a baby that probably starved to death when it was just a month or two old. It would have weighed about 88 pounds (40 kg).

Your Questions Answered

The main way that scientists find out amazing facts about dinosaurs is that no matter how much they discover, it always leads them to ask new questions. With the help of incredible finds, as well as detailed research and new technologies, they are building up a more and more detailed picture of how dinosaurs used to live. Here are some fascinating questions paleontologists are now able to answer.

Why did some dinosaurs grow to be so big?

Sauropods were the largest land animals that have ever lived. The reason why they grew to be so huge is still unclear to scientists. During the Jurassic, there was a large amount of plants, so one theory says that their size was linked to the amount of food that was available. Another theory suggests that they were able to grow so big because these dinosaurs had hollow bones, which meant that their overall bodyweight was relatively low. Scientists are still researching possible reasons, but it is likely that the answer is a combination of these and other theories.

The blue whale is the largest creature on Earth today. It can support its weight because it lives in the water.

What is the biggest fossilized dinosaur bone ever found?

In 2012, an Argentinian farmer found the fossilized remains of the largest dinosaur ever to be discovered: *Patagotitan*. The bone that the farmer had initially found was its thighbone, or femur. The femur is the longest bone in the body, and this femur is the largest fossilized bone that has ever been found, at 8 feet (2.4 m) long. Its owner measured 130 feet (40 m) from its nose to the tip of its tail.

How is it possible to know the weight of a dinosaur?

Fossils can tell us a lot about an animal, but it is hard to understand how much it weighed, because a lot of the body parts have not been preserved. How much did the organs weigh? The muscles? How much fat did the animal have? This is why scientists often calculate the weight of a dinosaur using computer programs. These programs use complex formulas and have been developed by studying today's large animals and how their body weight relates to their skeleton.

By trying to calculate the weight of elephants based on skeletons, scientists have learned a lot about estimating the weight of large land animals.

What can fossilized footprints tell us about dinosaurs?

A lot of what we know today about the way dinosaurs used to behave comes from studying fossilized footprints. When scientists find whole tracks, or sets, of footprints, they can work out whether the dinosaur lived in herds or not and how it took care of its young. Depending on the spacing of the footprints, we can tell whether the dinosaur was running (footprints close together) or striding (footprints further apart). We can also use the size of a fossilized footprint to calculate the animal's height. So while fossilized body parts are important for us to understand the different dinosaur species that used to roam the Earth, it's the preserved footprints that help us understand how they lived, moved, and communicated.

In perfect conditions, footprints can fossilize and reveal much more about a dinosaur's life than its bones can.

Glossary

allosaur A large theropod with a long, narrow skull, usually with ornamental horns or crests.

bipedal Walking upright on the back legs.

Cretaceous period The time from 145 to 65 mya, and the third of the periods that make up the Mesozoic Era.

diplodocid A very long sauropod with relatively short legs.

fossil The remains of an animal or plant that died long ago, preserved in rock.

gastrolith A stone in the stomach that helps digestion.

herbivore A plant-eater.

Jurassic period The time from 206 to 145 mya, and the second of the periods that make up the Mesozoic Era.

Mesozoic Era The period of geological time from 251 to 65 million years ago.

mya Short for "millions of years ago."

ornithischian Describes dinosaurs with hip bones arranged like a bird's. All plant-eaters, they include ornithopods, marginocephalians, and thyreophorans.

osteoderm A lumpy scale on a reptile's skin.

paleontologist A scientist who studies fossils.

plate A protective, bony section on a reptile's skin.

predator An animal that hunts and eats other animals for food.

prey An animal that is hunted and eaten by other animals for food.

prosauropod A primitive sauropod.

quadrupedal Walking on all four legs.

saurischian Describes dinosaurs with hip bones arranged like a lizard's. They include the meat-eating theropods and plant-eating sauropods.

sauropod An enormous, long-necked, plant-eating saurischian dinosaur that walked on all fours.

serrated Having a notched, knife-like edge.

species One particular type of living thing. Members of the same species look similar and can produce offspring together.

spinosaur A specialist theropod with a long, narrow snout for eating fish.

synapsid A primitive mammal.

theropod A bipedal saurischian dinosaur with sharp teeth and claws.

Triassic period The time from 251 to 206 mya, and the first of the periods that make up the Mesozoic Era.

Further Information

BOOKS

Holtz, Thomas R. Jr. *Digging for Brachiosaurus.* North Mankato, MN: Capstone Press, 2015.

Hulick, Kathryn. *The Science of Dinosaurs.* Minneapolis, MN: Abdo Publishing, 2016.

Naish, Darren, and Paul Barrett. *Dinosaurs: How They Lived and Evolved.* Washington, DC: Smithsonian Books, 2016.

Rissman, Rebecca. *Brachiosaurus and Other Big Long-Necked Dinosaurs: The Need-to-Know Facts.* North Mankato, MN: Capstone Press, 2016.

WEBSITES

discoverykids.com/category/dinosaurs/
This Discovery Kids site has tons of awesome information about dinosaurs, plus lots of fun games and exciting videos!

kids.nationalgeographic.com/explore/nature/dinosaurs/
Check out this National Geographic Kids site to learn more about dinosaurs.

www.amnh.org/explore/ology/paleontology
This website by the American Museum of Natural History is filled with dinosaur quizzes, information, and activities!

Index